GREEK ISLAND MYTHS

PATMOS
ST. JOHN THE THEOLOGIAN

JILL DUDLEY

PUT IT IN YOUR POCKET SERIES
ORPINGTON PUBLISHERS

Published by
Orpington Publishers

Cover design and origination by
Creeds, Bridport, Dorset
01308 423411

Printed and bound in the UK by
Creeds

© Jill Dudley 2017

ISBN: 978-0-9935378-8-2

PATMOS

ST. JOHN THE THEOLOGIAN

As you approach Patmos, you first pass several small islands before you see the great crenellated stone fortress-like Monastery of St. John the Evangelist which crowns the hill behind the port. The monastery is surrounded by a cluster of small whitewashed houses which appear to prostrate themselves at its feet; this is Chora, and below Chora is the port of Skala. The island is volcanic and beautiful, a jewel in the blue Aegean sea, wrought with creeks and coves with the monastery like a dark gleaming pearl dominating it.

According to archaeological finds and modern scholarship, the island once had on it many pagan temples. The most predominant was that of the goddess Artemis, twin sister of Apollo; she was goddess of young things and hunting, and was once equated with the moon; her temple stood spectacularly where the Monastery of John the Theologian now stands. Coincidently, Ephesus, the city from which St. John was banished, was also a centre for the worship of Artemis. Her temple at Ephesus was one of the seven wonders of the ancient world.

It was believed that St. John had been asked by Jesus at his crucifixion to take care of his mother, and St. John had brought her to a place now known as Meryemana in the hills behind Ephesus where she spent her last days. St. John's Jewish-Christian monotheism, however, had so angered the Roman Emperor Domitian that he had tried to poison him. The story goes that St. John drank the lethal substance but remained unaffected by it. Enraged that the poison had failed, the emperor gave it to someone else who died instantly, proving St. John had immunity through his faith in God. Irate for being thwarted in this manner, the Emperor banished John to Patmos. It is said that at some stage he escaped from his banishment by floating on a cork.

St. John performed many miracles on Patmos. For example, legend has it that his prayers had brought the columns of a temple of Apollo tumbling down, killing the priests of Apollo. Such pious tales were useful for helping to win pagans over to the Christian faith. Another claimed that at the time of John's exile there had been a magician on Patmos whose name was Kynops. His forté had been the ability to bring back as apparitions to the bereaved those who had drowned at sea. St. John, however, went one better and brought a newly drowned child back to life. When this same magician had gone wading out to sea to retrieve yet another apparition, St. John's prayers caused the unfortunate man to be sucked down and drowned.

A rather more light-hearted miracle is recorded in the Acts of St. John in the Apocrypha (early Christian books not included in the the New Testament). While still at Ephesus St. John one night was overheard by his companions saying: "I say unto you, O bugs, behave yourselves, one and all, and leave your abode for this night and remain quiet in one place, and keep your distance from the servants of God." The next morning at dawn his companions saw a number of bugs standing outside the door where St. John was sleeping. When

he finally woke, he praised them for their obedience. Not until he had left the room were they seen running back to enjoy the comforts of his bed again.

From the port of Skala there is an ancient mule track which goes up to the Grotto of St. John, a cave where the voice of God came to St. John and his faithful scribe Prochoros who wrote down *Revelation* at his dictation. St. John's warning in *Revelation* against 'the Beast' (the emperor), 'the Harlot' (the Roman Empire) and 'the great Distress' (God's impending judgement) must have been alarming to pagans. Any one who refused to follow Christ was threatened with 'the lake that burns with fire and brimstone, which is the second death.' Before death, moreover, they could expect to suffer horribly because after the blowing of trumpets, from 'the shaft of the bottomless pit' would come smoke 'Then from the smoke… locusts'. In other words those who did not turn to Christ would be tortured with pain and would regret it for all eternity; those who remained pagan and worshipped 'the Beast', would at the time of Judgement be reaped with a great sickle and thrown into the 'great wine-press of the wrath of God.' The voice of God had issued from a triple fissure in the Grotto which is said to represent the Trinity. Here St. John spent his time in prayer, and here was where he slept. Today candles are lit before icons and there are wall paintings.

A bus takes visitors from the port up the road which spirals up the hillside to Chora and the monastery on the summit. Chora is a maze of cobbled, vaulted alleyways and huddled whitewashed houses with numerous small churches tucked away amongst them. The dark fortress walls of the monastery

rise from the small buildings at its feet. The monastery was founded in 1088 by Osios (Holy) Christodoulos, a deeply devout monk and ascetic. By diplomacy he managed to acquire Patmos in exchange for lands on the island of Kos; his purpose, as he himself put it, was to create a 'workshop of virtue'.

A small door in the fortress wall leads into a cobbled and whitewashed cloister with many large terra-cotta pots of bright flowers. The *katholikon* (monastery church) is impressive with its ornate gilded *iconostasis* (altar screen) with its seventeenth century icons. There are many silver multiple-armed candelabra with candles hanging from the ceiling, silver icon lamps, and a marble flagged floor. It is believed that marble from the original temple of Artemis which once stood there was incorporated into the entrance to the church.

In the monastery museum is a marble plaque inscribed in Greek which came from the temple of Artemis. It described Patmos as the 'loveliest island of the daughter of Leto which came up from the depth as a resting place of her wanderings'. This daughter was Artemis, who was born when Zeus, supreme god of the ancient world, loved Leto, an immortal Titaness, who became pregnant with twins by him. When Zeus' wife Hera learned about it, she was so angry that she forbade the earth to allow the birth to take place anywhere under the sun. Leto wandered far and wide searching for a place prepared to risk Hera's wrath by being willing to receive her. Zeus eventually requested his brother Poseidon's help, and he raised from the sea's depths the tiny island of Delos.* It is a nice thought that Patmos provided a resting place for Artemis' mother Leto while she was seeking a place for her confinement.

The plaque in the monastery museum also mentions the fact that Orestes, the only son of King Agamemnon* who had led the Greek army against the Trojans in the Trojan War only to return home to Mycenae to be murdered by his wife, once visited this temple of Artemis on Patmos. He came to give thanks for being rescued from the Furies (hideous winged women who tormented those guilty of heinous crime, especially against the ties of kinship). After his father had been murdered by his wife (his mother), Orestes consulted the Delphic oracle and was told to avenge his father's murder. It was after he had committed this matricide that Orestes was harassed mercilessly by the Furies.

With no respite from them, Orestes again consulted the Delphic oracle and was told to go to Athens and stand trial. It must have been after he was acquitted of murder that Orestes visited Patmos and gave thanks at the temple of Artemis for his deliverance from the Furies.

From the monastery there is an intricate network of cobbled, vaulted alleyways which lead to a small *plateia*. There a couple of tavernas are ready to refresh visitors. The maze of alleyways was originally designed to confuse pirates but it is said that many of the pirates who came to steal valuable icons and other treasures from the monastery, suddenly saw the light and became monks; only a few sailed away as sinners.

From the monastery heights the volcanic island spreads out like a piece of jigsaw puzzle with its two isthmuses, and its many intricate pebbled coves and bays. At night the cruise ships festooned with fairy-lights adorn the port. Patmos is an island of sobriety but also of celebration. To be there for the Vigil held on the eve of the feast-day of Osios Christodoulos, the founder of the monastery, is to witness the mystery of the *katholikon* with its multi-armed chandeliers of numerous candles casting light and shadow on its exquisite interior; it is to experience the Orthodox Church's ability to work on the five human senses: sight, hearing, taste, smell and touch.

From the window high above the altar during the Vigil you may see moonlight filtering in, reminding those who are interested that the site is where Artemis, who was at one time identified with the moon, once had her temple. Just as Apollo, her twin brother, had at one time been identified with the sun.

As the monastery is the first thing that strikes the visitor on arrival, so it is the last that is seen on departure, leaving an everlasting and indelible memory.

* Denotes a separate booklet on the subject.

SOME GODS BORN OF ZEUS

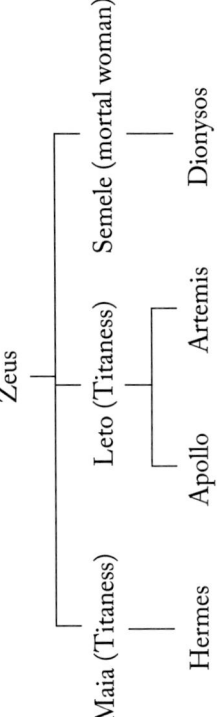

GLOSSARY OF GODS AND GODDESSES

APOLLO – Son of Zeus and the Titaness Leto. He was twin brother of Artemis, and god of medicine, music, archery and prophecy.

ARTEMIS – Daughter of Zeus and the Titaness Leto, and twin sister of Apollo. She was goddess of wild life, and defender of the very young. She was also goddess of hunting, and was once equated with the moon.

ATHENA – Daughter of Zeus. She was born mature and fully armed from his head. She was goddess of handicraft, and protectress of many cities, but especially Athens. She was also the embodiment of wisdom.

LETO – A Titaness who was loved by Zeus. She gave birth to twins, Apollo and Artemis.

POSEIDON – God of the sea and earthquakes, and often referred to as the 'earth-shaker'. He was brother of Zeus and Hera.

TITANS – The offspring of Ouranos (often spelt Uranus, the heavens) and Gaea (the earth). There were said to be twelve of them, six sons and six daughters. Kronos was one of the sons, and Rhea one of the daughters, and they were the parents of Zeus, Hera, Poseidon and other major Olympian gods.

ZEUS – Son of Kronos and Rhea. God of the heavens, and supreme god of the ancient world, and dispenser of justice. He was married to Hera.

MORE FROM THE
PUT IT IN YOUR POCKET SERIES

TROJAN WAR
THE JUDGEMENT OF PARIS
HELEN
KING AGAMEMNON
ACHILLES
THE WOODEN HORSE
ODYSSEUS

SACRED SITES
ATHENS – THE ACROPOLIS
CORINTH – ST. PAUL AND THE GODDESS OF LOVE
DELPHI – THE ORACLE OF APOLLO
ELEUSIS – DEMETER AND KORE
EPIDAURUS – CENTRE OF HEALING
OLYMPIA – THE OLYMPIC GAMES

ALSO BY JILL DUDLEY

YE GODS! (TRAVELS IN GREECE)

YE GODS! II (MORE TRAVELS IN GREECE)

LAP OF THE GODS (TRAVELS IN CRETE
AND THE AEGEAN ISLANDS)